The Soul Initiative for Eternity

"A Mission from God"

by Dr. Aaron R. Jones

The Soul Initiative for Eternity

A Mission from God

Dr. Aaron R. Jones

The Soul Initiative for Eternity
"A Mission from God"

Printed in the U.S.A.

Published by Kingdom Kaught Publishing, LLC

Copyright © 2015 by Dr. Aaron R. Jones

All rights reserved. No part of this book may be reproduced or transmitted in any form or by any means, electronic or mechanical, including photocopying, recording or by any information storage and retrieval system without written permission from the author, except for the inclusion of brief quotations in a review.

All scripture quotations are from the King James Version of the Bible. Thomas Nelson Publishers, Nashville: Thomas Nelson, Inc. 1972.

Editor: Sharon D. Jones

Copyediting: Sarah Gardner

Graphic Designer: JM Virtual Concepts

ISBN 9780996126731

Library of Congress Control Number: 2015953906

Table of Contents

INTRODUCTION 1

Principle #1 The Last Day Mentality 5

Principle #2 Calling the Watchman to Remove the Blood 13

Principle #3 Desperate for One 17

Principle #4 The Harvest is Ready 21

Principle #5 Redeem the Time 29

The Soul Initiative for Eternity Tools ... 33

   The Soul Initiative Group Facilitator . 35

   The Soul Commitment 37

   The Salvation Plan Card 39

   The Soul Attack Card 41

   The Soul Praise Report Card 43

   The Soul Prayer Request Card 45

   The Soul Letter 47

About the Author 49

INTRODUCTION

"For God so loved the world, that He gave His only begotten Son, that whosoever believeth in Him should not perish, but have everlasting life."
John 3:16

The purpose of The Soul Initiative for Eternity is to see that John 3:16 is fulfilled and that many individuals enter into a relationship with Jesus Christ. This relationship leads to everlasting (eternal) life.

Questions to ponder: Do you know where you will spend eternity? With whom will you spend eternity?

If your first answer is "yes" and your second is with the Heavenly Father, then you need to help someone else make this life-changing decision.

The Soul Initiative for Eternity

The Soul Initiative for Eternity is a mission to encourage and empower believers to reach lost souls. Lost souls are individuals who do not know and/or do not have a relationship with Jesus Christ.

The Soul Initiative is to bring evangelism and soul-winning to the forefront of every believer's heart and mind. We are living in a day where evangelism must be very intentional. Today, believers have taken such a laid back approach to soul-winning that evangelism seems like it is non-existent.

In the next few pages, we will look at five principles of the soul initiative for eternity:

1. The Last Day Mentality
2. Calling the Watchman to Remove the Blood
3. Desperate for One
4. The Harvest is Ready
5. Redeem the Time

The Soul Initiative for Eternity

The above principles should awaken the spirit man in all believers. This awakening will cause believers to reach the lost at any cost. Included with the five principles are some tools to help make soul-winning not just a concept, but a reality.

The Soul Initiative for Eternity

A Mission from God

Principle #1

THE LAST DAY MENTALITY

"This know also, that in the last days perilous times shall come. For men shall be lovers of their own selves, covetous, boasters, proud, blasphemers, disobedient to parents, unthankful, unholy, Without natural affection, trucebreakers, false accusers, incontinent, fierce, despisers of those that are good, Traitors, heady, highminded, lovers of pleasures more than lovers of God; Having a form of godliness, but denying the power thereof: from such turn away."
2 Timothy 3:1-5

The Soul Initiative for Eternity

We are truly living in the last days. The last days are the times between Jesus' first coming and second coming. The larger context, which Paul is speaking about, is the apostasy (turning away) of the Church. The heart and the mind of man are moving further away from God. Paul speaks of the mentality of man and the world today. He expresses the deep sin condition of mankind. Looking at the scriptures, we can see the desperate need for the Gospel for all mankind (souls).

Men shall be lovers of themselves.
- This world has become so self-centered and self-consumed, that God is pushed away and not even a topic in the life of man. Their whole life is centered around self (self-wants, self-desires, self-fulfillment). Paul provided a solution to this problem in

Philippians 2:3—*"Let nothing be done through strife or vainglory; but in lowliness of mind let each esteem other better than themselves."*

Man is covetous.
- The more man desires, the more man wants. The spirit of covet is having a strong desire for something that belongs to someone else. This spirit causes man to take things that are not his. Today, the rise in crime is in part because of covetousness. Man's methodology is to get all you can get by any means necessary. Exodus 20:17 addresses this spirit, *"Thou shalt not covet thy neighbour's house, thou shalt not covet thy neighbour's wife, nor his manservant, nor his maidservant, nor his ox, nor his ass, nor any thing that is thy neighbour's."*

Man is proud.

- Man has come to the conclusion that he does not need an Almighty God. He refuses to humble himself. He takes credit for all of his accomplishments. Man must realize without God he is nothing. Jesus says in John 15:5, ***"for without me ye can do nothing."***

Man is unthankful.

- Now-a-days, it is hard to hear "thank you" from people. So many people feel entitled to whatever is received. Man does not see the need to thank an awesome God. Being thankful is a sense of accountability. Being thankful to God keeps us accountable to Him. First Thessalonians 5:18 says, ***"In every thing give thanks: for this is the will of God in Christ Jesus concerning you."***

Man is unholy.

- The world has reached a new level of perversion. What was once was abnormal has become normal in family, television, and community. There is no shame, modesty, or discretion in the world. The world has taken on the mindset of corruption. Hebrews 12:14 says, **"Follow peace with all men, and holiness, without which no man shall see the Lord."**

Man loves pleasure more than God.

- Man has become enticed with life's pleasure. Man esteems his job, car, home, and other material things above God. The more man loves pleasures, the more he will dismiss the idea of having a relationship with God. Man's pleasures become his treasures. Jesus said in Matthew 6:19-21, **"Lay not up for yourselves treasures upon earth, where moth and rust doth corrupt,**

<u>and where thieves break through and steal: But lay up for yourselves treasures in heaven, where neither moth nor rust doth corrupt, and where thieves do not break through nor steal: For where your treasure is, there will your heart be also."</u>

Man has a form of godliness but denies the power of God.

- A form of godliness is performing actions that seem to honor God, but in reality the heart is not connected to Him. Man can appear religious, but the relationship is not manifested. In actuality, there isn't a real relationship with the Heavenly Father.

The last day mentality is where we are today. Man is totally consumed with himself and refuses to acknowledge God. This fact must not discourage or hinder one from witnessing to lost souls. We must apply the truth of the Gospel to this last day mentality.

Questions to ponder: Do you know anyone with the Last Day Mentality?

Are you witnessing as if Jesus were to return tomorrow?

A Mission from God

Principle #2

CALLING THE WATCHMAN TO REMOVE THE BLOOD

"Son of man, I have made thee a watchman unto the house of Israel: therefore hear the word at my mouth, and give them warning from me. When I say unto the wicked, Thou shalt surely die; and thou givest him not warning, nor speakest to warn the wicked from his wicked way, to save his life; the same wicked man shall die in his iniquity; but his blood will I require at thine hand. Yet if thou warn the wicked, and he turn not from his

wickedness, nor from his wicked way, he shall die in his iniquity; but thou hast delivered thy soul."
Ezekiel 3:17-19

This powerful scripture speaks to the heart of all believers. All believers are called to stand in the gap for a soul. Ezekiel was a prophet and had an awesome assignment. Ezekiel was a watchman of God's people. One called to be a watchman has the responsibility to protect individuals against any type of threat. The watchman was positioned in the best place to observe any danger. If a threat arose, the watchman would notify the city by sounding the appropriate alarm. Jeremiah 6:17 says, *"Also I set watchmen over you, saying, 'Hearken to the sound of the trumpet.' But they said, 'We will not hearken.' "*

God called and positioned Ezekiel to be a person to warn His people. Ezekiel did not have the option of seeing God's people go in the wrong direction as he looked away. Ezekiel had to warn the people of their ways and the imminent wrath of God.

God has called every believer to be a modern day watchman. Every day, a believer should wake up with a "watchman duty" in mind. Every believer should not take the luxury of turning his head and leaving a lost soul to try to figure out Who God Is. Daily, believers should never pass by people who are spiritually in danger. Satan's destruction agenda is found in John 10:10, *"The thief cometh not, but for to steal, and to kill, and to destroy: I am (Jesus) come that they might have life, and that they might have it more abundantly."*

God wants us to sound the alarm. Every day God places us in the best position to warn and sound the alarm. The message of warning is not our words, but God's Word. We must warn people in relation to the Gospel. No matter what the response is, we are required to give the warnings of God. God spoke directly to Ezekiel. God told him if he failed to warn the people of their ways and they died, the blood would be on his (Ezekiel's) hands. If Ezekiel is obedient to the warning of God and does what He says, and the people ignore the warning and dies, Ezekiel is released from the shed blood of the people. Believers, it is time to clear the blood off our hands, be obedient to God, and assume the role of a watchman.

Questions to ponder: Whose blood is on your hands? Are you sounding the alarm?

Principle #3

DESPERATE FOR ONE

"And he spake this parable unto them, saying, "What man of you, having an hundred sheep, if he lose one of them, doth not leave the ninety and nine in the wilderness, and go after that which is lost, until he find it? And when he hath found it, he layeth it on his shoulders, rejoicing. And when he cometh home, he calleth together his friends and neighbours, saying unto them, Rejoice with me; for I have found my sheep which was lost. I say unto you, that likewise joy shall be in heaven over one sinner that repenteth,

more than over ninety and nine just persons, which need no repentance."
Luke 15:3-7

We must never forsake the one (lost soul). One can be a powerful multiplier when you keep adding them. Before a thousand souls can be reached, one soul must be reached. Just think about the person that led Billy Graham or T.D. Jakes to Jesus Christ. They were just one, but at this point thousands have come to Christ because of their ministry.

Jesus gives a parable. A parable is a natural story that leads to spiritual understanding. This parable is one of three that focuses on the one. It shows how God views the one.

Jesus talks about a shepherd (man) having one hundred sheep. He loses one and goes out of the way to find the one. The shepherd actually left the ninety-nine sheep to recover the one. This is an important point, he left the ninety-nine to go get the one. Why is the one important? Please understand that the ninety-nine (the present believers) are very important. In Ephesians 4:11-12, Paul makes clear the need for all believers in the body of Christ: *"And he gave some, apostles; and some, prophets; and some, evangelists; and some, pastors and teachers; For the perfecting of the saints, for the work of the ministry, for the edifying of the body of Christ:"* However, the problem is that most churches have become so focused on edifying themselves (the ninety-nine), they have caused the one to become a "none" factor.

When the shepherd saw that the sheep was missing, he did not allow the fact that the ninety-nine were okay stop him from seeking after the one. He made a diligent search. We must have this same passion for the one who is lost.

The Soul Initiative for Eternity

What drives the love of Christ should be our drive. When we see a lost soul, that lost soul should be important to us. Our commitment to that one soul should be indescribable. Sharing the Good News of Jesus Christ should be our motivation. Most importantly, you desire to see the lost soul found in Christ. You no longer want to see the lost soul headed to eternal separation from God. Believers should understand that one soul makes a difference to God. Will you be the agent of multiplication for the Kingdom of God? Just as you live one day at a time, you should reach one soul at a time. Remember you were that one that someone came back to reach for the Kingdom of God.

Question to ponder: Is there one person you know you need to reach today?

Principle #4

THE HARVEST IS READY

"And Jesus went about all the cities and villages, teaching in their synagogues, and preaching the gospel of the kingdom, and healing every sickness and every disease among the people. But when he saw the multitudes, he was moved with compassion on them, because they fainted, and were scattered abroad, as sheep having no shepherd. Then saith he unto his disciples, "The harvest truly is plenteous, but the labourers are few; Pray ye therefore the Lord of the

harvest, that He will send forth labourers into his harvest."
Matthew 9:35-38

What is going to turn the world upside down and reach the soul for the Kingdom? The answer is very simple, **more laborers**. The plentiful harvest is about lost souls. A plentiful harvest is a harvest that is ready. When Jesus looked at the harvest, He said it was plentiful. He was saying, "There are many."

Jesus did not see the harvest as an inconvenience. He was concerned about the soul. The harvest being plentiful will never go away. It is a reality until Jesus comes back for His Church. The believer is responsible for reaching the harvest. We cannot be followers of Jesus Christ and just look at the harvest, we must take action. The harvest should compel believers to do something.

The Soul Initiative for Eternity

The Church has become full of Christians, but God is still looking at the harvest and the un-churched. There are 5 approaches that Jesus has given the believer in order to reach the harvest: help, love, pray, send, and go.

Help

A part of witnessing to the lost soul is fulfilling (helping with) needs. Jesus saw the needs and fulfilled them. Those that were sick Jesus healed, which confirmed His role as the Messiah. Jesus met individual immediate needs. Today, we understand that needs can be spiritual, emotional, and physical. Matthew 25:35-36 says, *"For I was an hungred, and ye gave me meat: I was thirsty, and ye gave me drink: I was a stranger, and ye took me in: Naked, and ye clothed me: I was sick, and ye visited me: I was in prison, and ye came unto me."*

Love

When you see a lost soul, what do you see? Jesus' heart was moved with compassion because He saw the people's spiritual condition. They had no one to guide, teach, or cover them. The worse of it all is that they did not know they were lost. Why was Jesus telling His disciples about the harvest? He wanted His disciples to have the same compassion as He had. He not only wanted them to have the compassion, but also the understanding of the lost. The motivation for Jesus' ministry was the lost. Luke 19:10 says, *"For the Son of man is come to seek and to save that which was lost."*

Pray

Romans 10:1 says, *"Brethren, my heart's desire and prayer to God for Israel is, that they might be saved."* A believer's prayer time just cannot be consumed with his life's problems and situations. He must step outside of himself, and pray for the lives of those who are headed to an eternal separation from God. Lost souls should be a part of our prayer lives. The unsaved soul should be on your lips as a heartfelt cry.

Pray to God that you will become an active vessel used to help bring souls to the Kingdom. Pray that the Holy Spirit moves you to be a witness. Pray that doors of opportunities are open, so you can seize the moment. Pray that God gives you a greater love for the lost. Pray that God will give you an unending burden for the lost. Pray to view lost souls as Christ did.

Send

The Church must send missionaries and evangelism teams to reach the harvest. This is a method to spread the Gospel of Jesus Christ. This sending must be moved by the Holy Spirit. Acts

13:2 says, *"As they ministered to the Lord, and fasted, the Holy Ghost said, 'Separate me Barnabas and Saul for the work whereunto I have called them.'"*

There was a time that the United States was known to send missionaries all over the world. Today, missionaries from other countries are being sent to the United States. The United States is looked upon as being a mission field. The Church has to be actively sending men and women out to spread the Gospel of Jesus Christ. The Church needs to flood communities with the message of Jesus Christ. Can the Church choose to focus on soul-winning before it hosts another program, event, or fundraiser?

Go

There are some who have been called to help, love, pray, and send; but there are others who must go. Matthew 28:19, 20 says, *"Go ye therefore, and teach all nations, baptizing them in the name of the Father, and of the Son, and of the Holy Ghost: Teaching them to observe all things whatsoever I have commanded you: and, lo, I am with you always, even unto the end of the world. Amen."*

God is calling all believers to go out and reach a lost soul. God has sent out a special invitation and we must respond and take on the challenge like Isaiah. Isaiah 6:8 says, *"Also I heard the voice of the Lord, saying, 'Whom shall I send, and who will go for us? Then said I, Here am I; send me.' "* Today is the day to GO!!!

Questions to Ponder: Are you going to look at the harvest day-end and day-out and do absolutely nothing? Are you going to allow the Words of Jesus to fall to the ground? What role will you play today (help, love, pray, send, or go) for the lost souls?

The Soul Initiative for Eternity

A Mission from God

Principle #5

REDEEM THE TIME

"See then that ye walk circumspectly, not as fools, but as wise. Redeeming the time, because the days are evil."
Ephesians 5:15, 16

Today is the day you will witness to someone who doesn't know Jesus. Do not miss the opportunity. Redeem the Time!! Stop complaining and stressing over the souls you may have missed. It is time to be a Good Samaritan. Will you purpose in your heart to no longer walk by a spiritually-wounded soul? Stop and help with the healing process. Luke 10:30-37 says,

The Soul Initiative for Eternity

And Jesus answering said, "A certain man went down from Jerusalem to Jericho, and fell among thieves, which stripped him of his raiment, and wounded him, and departed, leaving him half dead. And by chance there came down a certain priest that way: and when he saw him, he passed by on the other side. And likewise a Levite, when he was at the place, came and looked on him, and passed by on the other side. But a certain Samaritan, as he journeyed, came where he was: and when he saw him, he had compassion on him, And went to him, and bound up his wounds, pouring in oil and wine, and set him on his own beast, and brought him to an inn, and took care of him. And on the morrow when he departed, he took out two pence, and gave them to the host, and said unto him, Take care of him; and whatsoever thou spendest more, when I come again, I will repay thee. Which now of these three, thinkest thou, was neighbour unto him that fell among the thieves? And he said, He that shewed mercy on him.

The Soul Initiative for Eternity

Then said Jesus unto him, Go, and do thou likewise."

Questions to Ponder: Will you no longer be judgmental and reach that wounded soul? Will you leave that soul to die? Will you redeem the time and help him/her know Jesus?

The Soul Initiative for Eternity

A Mission from God

THE SOUL INITIATIVE FOR ETERNITY TOOLS

Now you are ready to apply what you know is the Divine assignment for your life. The following tools can be used individually or corporately. This is good for small groups.

The Soul Initiative for Eternity

A Mission from God

THE SOUL INITIATIVE GROUP FACILITATOR

- Should have read the entire The Soul Initiative for Eternity
- Should have at least one Soul Attack Card
- Ensures that every name listed on the Soul Attack Cards is mentioned in prayer
- Ensures the Soul Group stays focused on the souls listed on the Soul Attack Card
- Ensures that the Soul Group time doesn't lead to ungodly conversation about any soul listed on the Soul Attack Card

The Soul Initiative for Eternity

A Mission from God

THE SOUL COMMITMENT

I commit to praying for lost souls daily.

I commit to being obedient to God when He leads me to a lost soul.

I commit to making lost souls a priority in my life.

I commit to looking for opportunities to witness the Gospel of Jesus Christ.

I commit to support churches, ministries, and organizations that send missionaries out to build the Kingdom of God.

I commit to be faithful to my Soul Attack List.

The Soul Initiative for Eternity

This commitment I make to my
Heavenly Father

This _____ day of _____
20__

_____

Signature of the Believer Making the
Commitment

_____

Signature of a Witness

THE SALVATION PLAN CARD

This card should be with you at all times. This card will help you to be intentional about witnessing to a lost soul. This card will help you present the Salvation Plan to an individual.

The Soul Initiative for Eternity

"A Mission for God"

The Salvation Plan (Romans 10:9-10)

[1] Confess Jesus as Lord
[2] Believe in your heart that Jesus died on the cross and rose from the dead.
[3] Accept Jesus as Lord and Savior of your life.

The Soul Initiative for Eternity

A Mission from God

THE SOUL ATTACK CARD

This card should be close by, and viewed daily. This card will help you to be intentional about praying for specific lost souls.

The Soul Initiative for Eternity

"A Mission for God"

ATTACK CARD

Today's Date: _____

[1] _____ _____
[2] _____ _____
[3] _____ _____
[4] _____ _____
[5] _____ _____

I commit to the above names that I will pray, contact, and do all I can to help them accept Jesus Christ as Lord and Savior.

The Soul Initiative for Eternity

A Mission from God

THE SOUL PRAISE REPORT CARD

This card will help you to be intentional about celebrating the conversion of a soul.

The Soul Initiative for Eternity

"A Mission for God"

SOUL PRAISE REPORT

Today's Date _____

Name _____ _____
_____
_____
_____
_____
_____
_____
_____

This card is used to record praise reports of all souls connected to the Body of Christ.

The Soul Initiative for Eternity

A Mission from God

THE SOUL PRAYER REQUEST CARD

This card should be close by, and viewed daily. This card will help you to be intentional about praying for specific needs of each lost soul.

The Soul Initiative for Eternity

"A Mission for God"

PRAYER REQUEST CARD

Today's Date _____

Name _____ _____

_____
_____
_____
_____
_____
_____
_____

The card will be used for the prayer needs of the individuals on my Soul Attack Card.

The Soul Initiative for Eternity

A Mission from God

THE SOUL LETTER

Dear _____:

This a short letter to let you know that you have been in my thoughts and prayers. God has led me to put your name on my Soul Attack List. This list is simply names of people God loves and wants to have an eternal relationship. I have committed daily to pray for you, to hear your heart, and to do what it takes, so you would accept Jesus Christ as your Lord and Savior. My prayer is that you will see the joy of having a true relationship with Jesus Christ. This does not mean I will be judgmental or harsh, but I will be the person talking to God about you.

The Soul Initiative for Eternity

I love you, but I know God loves you more. That is why He placed your name on my heart. If you are reading this letter and you want to make a real change in your life today, call or text me. Do what you have to reach me. I close with Romans 10:9-10

"That if thou shalt confess with thy mouth the Lord Jesus, and shalt believe in thine heart that God hath raised him from the dead, thou shalt be saved.

For with the heart man believeth unto righteousness; and with the mouth confession is made unto salvation."

For your eternity,

_____

About the Author

Dr. Aaron R. Jones serves as Senior Pastor of New Hope Church of God. Under his pastorate is New Hope Kiddie Kollege, Inc (Daycare) and New Hope Community Outreach Services, Inc. Dr. Jones also oversees New Hope Church of God Ghana and New Hope Church of God Uganda.

Dr. Jones is an Ordained Bishop with the Church of God denomination and is the DELMARVA-DC District Overseer (14 churches). Dr. Jones serves on DELMARVA-DC's State Council, Ministerial Internship Program Board, Urban Ministry Committee, Finance Committee, and Chaplain's Board. He also serves on both the Church of God's International and DELMARVA-DC Ministry to the Military Board. In his local community, Dr. Jones serves as a Chaplain for the Charles County Sheriff Department and Chairman of the Hospice of Charles County, Inc. Chaplain's Advisory Board. Dr. Jones also serves on the Board of Directors for William Seymour College.

Being obedient to 2 Timothy 2:15, *"Study to show thyself approved…"* Dr. Jones received a Doctorate in Theology and Pastoral Counseling from Life Christian University and a Doctorate in Christian Counseling from American Christian College and Seminary. He is a certified Pastoral Counselor with the International Association of Christian Counseling Professionals. He is the former Executive Vice President of the National Bible College and Seminary in Fort Washington, Maryland.

Dr. Jones has published eight books that provide a biblical foundation for Christian doctrine and discipline: *The*

Disciples Conclusion; The Disciples Conclusion Workbook; The Joshua Resolution; Out of My Comfort Zone to Honor God; The Pastor's Intercessor; How the Holy Trinity Communicates to Mankind+; Eight Effective Keys to Personal Evangelism; and Equipping the Church for the Harvest. He is the founder and owner of God's Comfort Ministries, LLC, which provides Christian literature, evangelism training, and spiritual guidance.

Dr. Jones not only serves God, but his country as well. He has served over 20 years in the Armed Forces. He is a retired Chaplain with the Army National Guard. He participated in both Operation Noble Eagle (2003) and Operation Iraqi Freedom III (2005).

Pastor Jones is happily married to the former Sharon Russell. He sincerely believes without her love, support, and encouragement, many of his goals would not have been accomplished.

www.ingramcontent.com/pod-product-compliance
Lightning Source LLC
Chambersburg PA
CBHW070552300426
44113CB00011B/1879